CH00585334

Ludwig Grieser

# Healthy Recipes for Sea and Freshwater

# Fish

Cookery Editor Sonia Allison

Series Editor Wendy Hobson

*foulsham*

# Foreword

In any good cookery book, the chapter on preparing fish dishes is one of the most exciting. Imagine wandering around an outdoor market on a summer's day in France, Italy, Spain, Portugal or even at home for that matter. The variety of freshwater and sea fish on offer at the fish stall or counter can be irresistible, with such an assortment of shapes, sizes and colours to choose from. The fresh vegetable and herb stands complete the picture and you can let your imagination run wild just thinking about all the delicious meals you could prepare. It was with this image in mind that this book has been put together, and it contains a collection of some of the recipes that have proved most popular in my restaurant. What was once a hobby is now a career, and my special interest is in cooking fish and seafood dishes.

# Contents

# The Wealth of Freshwater and Sea Fish

Any keen cook will enjoy preparing fish dishes. To achieve the best results it is important to remember that the fish should be as fresh as possible but it does not have to be the most expensive. You will also need to put a certain amount of time and care into the preparation.

# Fish and Nutrition

Fish is right in fashion, and gourmets, nutritionists and creative cooks cannot speak too highly of its virtues.

It has provided a healthy source of food for thousands of years. For a long time it was only enjoyed by people who lived close to the coasts, rivers or lakes while those living inland ate fish only during Lent. River fish has not always been popular because of the bones. It is only in recent times that attitudes have changed as it is nearly always served filleted.

Improvements in transport, refrigeration and packaging bring freshly-caught fish directly to our shops and supermarkets. Any large town or city can boast at least one well stocked fishmonger who will sell the popular cod and haddock as well as the more expensive fish such as sole and turbot.

As fish is easy to digest and has a relatively low fat content, it should be eaten regularly as part of a healthy, balanced diet. Illnesses related to heart disease are less common amongst the Japanese and Eskimos. This is often attributed to the fact that their fish consumption is well above average and fish contains a high proportion of unsaturated fatty acids which are now said to combat heart disease.

The consumption of fish is rising all the time and demand is already exceeding supply for fish caught in the wild. The increasing pollution of the seas and the steady decline of the number of fish in the wild has meant that fish farms are becoming a more common source of supply. They are able to supply fish that is always of a similar standard and is readily available.

This book cannot mention every one of the wide variety of fish available, but it will give you a range of varied and delicious recipes to win you over to or confirm your opinion of the delights of fish.

# About the Recipes

1 Do not mix metric, Imperial or American measures. Follow one set only.

2 Spoon measurements are level.

3 Eggs are size 3.

4 Kcals and kJs given are approximate and refer to one portion.

5 Preparation times include both preparation and cooking times and are approximate.

6 Temperatures given are for conventional ovens. Lower temperatures may be sufficient for fan-assisted ovens so consult the manufacturer's handbook.

# Freshwater Fish

**Salmon** ①
Salmon and trout belong to the salmonidae family. They are easily recognised by a stubby adipose fin between the dorsal and tail fin. The salmon has a long body with a lot of small scales and an extended jaw with sharp teeth. It is a migratory fish, spending about the first two years of its life in the rivers before travelling to the sea. A few years later it returns to the rivers to spawn. The quality of wild Atlantic and Pacific salmon used to be better than farmed fish, but improved methods of farming salmon have made it

difficult to tell the difference. The fish are usually between 40 and 60 cm (16 and 24 in) in length, though can be much bigger, and weigh an average of 3 to 6 kg (7 to 14 lb).

Salmon flesh is rich-tasting, delicate and flaky and is characteristically pinky-orange in colour.

Salmon can be smoked, poached, grilled, pickled or used in pâtes, mousses and purées.

**Trout**
There are three kinds of this very popular freshwater fish: brook trout (1)

are frequently caught by anglers but are not otherwise readily available; rainbow trout (2) are the most common variety, and usually come from fish farms; salmon trout (3) are migratory fish, like the salmon.

Trout can be smoked, fried, grilled, braised or cooked *au bleu* (see page 16).

**Pike** ⑤
This voracious predatory fish has a long body, a large bill-shaped mouth and sharp fangs. Its flesh is white, lean and firm, but unfortunately it has a lot of bones. Pike is at its best

7

when it is under two years old, weighing about 2 kg (4½ lb).

Pike can be poached, fried and baked, but is best when made into quenelles (see page 19).

## Carp ⑥

There are three different kinds of carp: the king carp, the mirror carp and the leather carp. These are distinguished by their scales. Carp live in ponds and slow-flowing waters. The mirror carp is the most popular kind as it is bred in fish farms for its good, lean flesh. The fish usually weighs between 1 and 3 kg (2 and 7 lb). Anglers should leave their catch in clear, fresh water for a few days before killing them.

Carp can be baked, braised, stewed and cooked *au bleu* (see page 16).

## Tench

Tench is a tasty fish found in still or gently flowing waters. As with carp, anglers should leave it in fresh water for a few days before killing.

Tench can be cooked *au bleu* (see page 16), in fish soups and stews. The barbel can be prepared in the same way.

## Catfish ⑦

Another predatory fish, these live in lakes and large rivers and have two long feelers on the upper jaw and four shorter ones on the underside. When the fish is young, its flesh is white, tasty and has few bones. However, it is a little fatty.

Catfish can be braised, grilled or smoked.

## Perch ⑧

This is another prized predatory fish with a firm, white, lean flesh.

Perch can be poached, braised or fried, or whole fish can be stuffed or baked in salt pastry (see page 50).

## Eel ⑨

The eel spends its early life in fresh water and goes to the sea to spawn. It should be skinned before purchase as the skin is very thick.

Eel can be braised, grilled or smoked.

# Sea Fish

### Herring ⑩
One of the most popular fish, the herring's body is slim and silvery and has a short dorsal fin. The flesh is tasty and rich in healthy oil. Herring live in large shoals in the northern hemisphere.

Herring can be pickled, smoked, grilled, fried, baked or soused.

### Cod ⑪
This very common fish from the North Sea and the Atlantic has very lean, tender and flaky flesh. It can be between 60 and 100 cm (24 and 40 in) long and weighs between 5 and 8 kg (11 and 18 lb).

Cod can be poached, braised, fried or baked.

### Haddock ⑫
Another member of the large cod family, the haddock is easily identified by a black blotch above the pectoral fin and a black line running along its side. It lives mostly in the North Atlantic and the Arctic Sea and has firm, lean flesh.

Haddock can be boiled, poached, fried or baked.

### Pollack ⑬
Although this is another tasty member of the cod family, it is not very popular as an everyday fish. It comes from the North Atlantic and is frequently canned and used as a substitute for salmon. It is also dried.

Pollack can be used in fish soups, stews and stuffings or fried.

### Whiting ⑭
The whiting is a long, small fish. It is a greenish colour on top and its sides are a shiny silver. It lives in the North Atlantic, the North Sea and the Baltic and is an excellent, versatile fish.

Whiting can be poached, baked or fried, and the fillets can be used in soups and stews.

### Red Sea Bass
This fish comes from the northern hemisphere and has sharp spines on its

dorsal fin. Its flesh is a pale pink colour and it tastes extremely good. It is usually only sold as fillets.

Red sea bass can be baked, fried or poached.

## Mackerel ⑮
Mackerel is a greenish-blue fish shaped like a torpedo with black stripes along its back. It is found in the Mediterranean, the Atlantic, the North Sea and the Baltic and is usually about 25 to 30 cm (10 to 12 in) long. The flesh is oily, firm and flavoursome and it has few bones.

Mackerel can be smoked, marinated, grilled, fried or poached.

## Monkfish ⑯
A predatory fish from the Mediterranean and the Atlantic, the monkfish can be dark brown or black in colour and has a large ugly head. Its flesh is white and firm with a delicate flavour and it has no bones.

Monkfish is best fried, but can also be grilled, braised or used in soups and stews.

## John Dory ⑰
This oval, flat fish has a pronounced spine on its dorsal fin and is distinguished by black spots on both sides. It is a fine-tasting fish from the Mediterranean and the Atlantic; however there is a lot of waste when it is filleted and this makes it very expensive.

John Dory can be fried,

grilled or braised and served with a sauce.

## Redfish ⑱
At home in the Mediterranean or the Atlantic, this fish is red in colour with a large head and spiky dorsal fin, so it must be handled with care. The flesh is firm and very tasty.

Redfish is a classic bouillabaisse fish, but it can also be poached, or stuffed and stewed.

## Gurnard ⑲
This bony fish has a bill-shaped mouth and can be red or grey. It lives in the Mediterranean (the red kind) and the Atlantic and its flesh is lean and firm.

Gurnard is best in bouillabaisse, braised or fried.

## Sea Bass or Loup de Mer ⑳
Another member of the bass family, this fish is greyish-blue and shimmering silver in colour. Its

front fins consist of spines. It is found in the Mediterranean and the Atlantic. As it has delicious, firm, white flesh it is currently very popular although very expensive when compared to other fish.

The wolf-fish (21) is similar to the sea bass and the two are often confused.

Sea bass can be steamed, fried or grilled, or is excellent baked in salt pastry. It is popular in Chinese cookery.

## Gold Bream 22

The most coveted of all bream, there are also red bream, tooth bream and sea bream. The gold bream is distinguished by its mother-of-pearl stripes between its big eyes. It lives in the Mediterranean, the Atlantic and off the coast of Africa and feeds on crustaceans and small squids.

Bream can be braised, stewed or fried and served with a sauce.

## Red Mullet

Also called red snapper, this fine fish is easily recognised by two feelers on its lower jaw. It comes from the Mediterranean and the Black Sea and can be up to 30 cm (12 in) long.

Mullet can be grilled or fried, or the fillets can be braised and served with a light sauce.

## Tuna Fish 24

Tuna fish are found in all the seas and play a particularly important role in the economy of the USA and Japan. There are three different kinds: red tuna, the slightly smaller white tuna which tastes the best, and bonito tuna which is the smallest. They all have firm, slightly oily flesh and are full of vitamins.

Tuna can be grilled, braised in olive oil or marinated. Most tuna is canned.

## Halibut 25

This is the biggest of the flat fish. It lives in all the northern seas and can grow to 3 m (about 3¼ yards) long. However, the smaller fish taste better, so the large ones are not sold in the shops. It has white flesh and is very high in protein. There is also a black halibut that is inferior in quality and is usually only sold as fillets.

Halibut can be cut into

slices and poached or grilled.

## Turbot

The most coveted and therefore also the most expensive of the flat fish, turbot is to be found in the Mediterranean and the Atlantic. It can adapt its colouring to its surroundings. The best fish stock is made from its head and bones. It usually weighs between 2 and 4 kg (4½ and 9 lb) although baby turbots are also available.

Turbot can be grilled, poached, braised or used in mousses and pâtés.

## Plaice

This is the smallest kind of flat fish and is mostly caught in the North Sea, the Baltic and the Atlantic. It is readily available in the shops. It is dark grey or brown in colour with orange spots. The flesh is white and quite rich-tasting. A normal weight for a plaice would be anything from 225 to 450 g (8 oz to 1 lb).

Plaice is usually fried, but can also be grilled, baked or steamed.

## Sole

Alongside the turbot, this is another of the tastiest and most popular flat fish. It lives in the North Sea, the Atlantic and the Mediterranean and has fine, white, firm flesh. It also tends to be fairly expensive.

Sole can be fried, grilled, braised or fillets can be poached.

# Buying and Preparation

It is most important to use fish that is absolutely fresh. When buying freshwater fish, it may be possible in some areas to buy it from fishmongers who keep the fish alive in tanks until they are bought.

There are certain signs to look for in sea fish:

the gills should be bright red and the structure should be intact;

the skin should be shiny and undamaged, and any remaining slime should be clear;

the eyes should be bright and shiny and should protrude slightly;

the smell should be pleasant;

the scales should be shiny and remain in place;

the cavity should be clean and have virtually no smell;

any remaining blood

should be red;

if any parasites (nematodes) are present, they should be visible to the naked eye on close inspection.

It is worth remembering the following motto: 'It is better to buy an absolutely fresh cod than a four day old sole.'

## Removing the scales

1 Hold the fish firmly by the tail and scrape the scales off with the back of a knife. It is best to do this in the sink as otherwise the scales will fly everywhere and make a dreadful mess.

2 Finally rinse the fish and

pat dry with kitchen paper.

## Gutting a Fish

1 Using a small sharp knife, cut along the underside of the fish from the tail to the throat. Do not cut too deeply or you may damage the gall bladder.

2 Pull out the innards and cut off at the head end.

3 Remove any remaining blood and the hose-shaped kidneys which lie directly under the main bones. Use a spoon handle or thumb nail.

4 Rinse the stomach and mouth cavities with cold water. If you are planning to cook your fish *au bleu* (see page 16), take care not to damage the slimy

skin as this gives the fish its characteristic blue colour in cooking.

## Filleting a Round Fish

**1** When filleting any round fish, start by removing the head. Place the fish on a board with the stomach facing you and cut behind the gills with a sharp knife until you get through to the bone.

**2** Turn the fish around and do the same on the other side. Press hard with the knife to cut through the bone.

**3** Release the top fillet by running a knife from the head to the tail end along the bones. Turn the fish over and release the second fillet by cutting along the bones.

**4** Remove any remaining bones and fins with a small sharp knife.
**5** The skin can now be removed from the fillet by cutting from the tail end, applying light pressure all the way down.
**6** The bones in freshwater fish can be removed with pincers or tweezers. Both the fillets should be rinsed quickly in cold water, (they should not be left in water) and patted dry with kitchen paper.

## Filleting a Flat Fish

**1** Cut the fish down the middle, following the line of the bone from head to tail.

**2** Next cut along each side from the head to the back and down the edges of the fins up to the main bone.

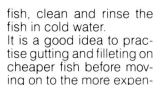

fish, clean and rinse the fish in cold water.
It is a good idea to practise gutting and filleting on cheaper fish before moving on to the more expensive ones.

**3** Starting from the middle, ease out the bones with the aid of a sharp, flexible knife and release the top fillet.

**2** Pull the rest of the skin off with your hands, holding the tail with a cloth and pulling towards the head. Turn the sole round and do the same with the other side.

## Skinning a Sole

**4** Release the second fillet in the same way. You may come across the roe sack; do not damage it as it can be used in speciality fish dishes.

**1** Dip the end of the tail fin into boiling water for a few minutes and then start to peel the skin off with a knife.

**3** Remove the head with a sharp knife and cut off the fins with kitchen shears.
**4** Any remaining blood, roes etc. should be removed and the sole rinsed in cold water.

**5** Turn the fish over and release both the fillets as described above.
**6** Remove the skin in the same way as for round

# Basic Recipes

Fish should never be cooked at high temperature as the flesh will toughen and dry out and the delicate flavour will be destroyed. Careful, gentle cooking is important in the success of any fish dish (except for frying).

## Poaching and Steaming

These are two of the best methods of cooking fish. Fish can be poached in salted water, a fish stock or court bouillon. This method is particularly suitable for large, whole fish in their skins. Poached fillets are best served swimming in a little of the cooking stock. In both cases the stock should be hot but not boiling.

The same method is used to cook trout or tench *au bleu*, but the fish has a little white wine vinegar poured over it just before poaching which gives the skin its blue colour.

Fish is steamed by cooking it in a steamer over slightly salted simmering water that has been flavoured with herbs and/or root vegetables.

## Deep Frying

This is especially popular in the Mediterranean and similar hot countries. Small whole fish or fillets are coated in flour, breadcrumbs or batter and are immersed in hot oil. It is important to use the best quality cooking oil and to drain afterwards on kitchen paper.

## Baking

This method is used predominantly in cooking whole fish, which may be encased in pastry, salt pastry or foil. The fish may be flavoured or stuffed with herbs or other flavourings and baked in a covered ovenproof dish to maintain the delicate flavours.

## Braising and Stewing

Fish can be braised in its own juices with a little butter, shallots, root vegetables, a few tablespoons of wine, fish stock or water. The fish is baked in a pan with an airtight lid at a low heat.

Fish can be stewed in the same way, when it should be left uncovered and carefully watched to prevent overcooking.

# Shallow Frying

This is one of the best known ways of cooking fish and is most suited to small whole fish or fillets. The fish may be coated in flour but any superfluous flour should be dusted off. The best results are achieved by frying in a mixture of butter and sunflower oil.

# Grilling

This method works well with small fish or slices of larger fish but it is important to make sure the grill does not become too hot. The fish should not be cooked too close to the source of heat and it is a good idea to lay the fish on aluminium foil.

# Fish Stock

Makes about 1 l/1³/₄ pt/4 ¹/₄ cups
Preparation time: 60 mins

---

1 kg/2¹/₄ *lb bones, head and trimmings of sole, plaice or turbot*

25 g/1 *oz*/2 tbsp butter or olive oil

2 onions, finely chopped

100 g/*4 oz* leeks, finely chopped

100 g/*4 oz* celery, finely chopped

4 ripe tomatoes, chopped

1 sprig thyme, finely chopped

3 sprigs parsley, finely chopped

1 bay leaf

250 ml/*8 fl oz*/1 cup dry white wine

1 l/1³/₄ *pts*/4 ¹/₄ cups water

---

**1** Wash and chop up the fish trimmings. Brown for about 10 minutes in butter or olive oil with the finely chopped vegetables and herbs.
**2** Pour in the wine and cold water, bring to the boil and leave the stock to simmer gently for about 30 minutes, skimming it frequently. Simmer the stock very gently or it will not remain clear.
**3** Strain the stock and leave to cool.

---

**Gourmet Tip**
Fish stock can be frozen for up to 4 weeks, after which it loses some of its flavour. Pour the cooked stock into ice-cube containers and, when they are frozen, store them in plastic bags. This means that you will always have small quantities ready to use.

## Court Bouillon

Makes about 1 l/1¾ pts/4 ¼ cups
Preparation time: 40 mins

*1 onion, finely chopped*

*½ leek, finely chopped*

*1 small carrot, finely chopped*

*¼ stick celery, finely chopped*

*500 ml/18 fl oz/2¼ cups water*

*500 ml/18 fl oz/2¼ cups good quality dry white wine*

*2 sprigs parsley*

*1 sprig thyme*

*1 bay leaf*

*5 white peppercorns*

*15 ml/1 tbsp sea salt*

**1** Put the finely chopped vegetables, water, wine, herbs and salt into a saucepan. Bring to the boil and simmer for about 30 minutes. Strain.
**2** Cool to lukewarm before using.

## Saffron Cream Sauce

Makes about 250 ml/8 fl oz/1 cup
Preparation time: 30 mins

*2 tbsp shallots, finely chopped*

*5 strands saffron*

*75 g/3 oz/⅓ cup salted butter*

*45 ml/3 tbsp dry vermouth*

*90 ml/6 tbsp fish stock (see page 17)*

*200 ml/7 fl oz/scant 1 cup single cream*

*a few drops of Pernod*

*white pepper*

*a few drops of lemon juice*

**1** Cook the shallots and saffron strands gently in the butter until softened, then pour in the vermouth and fish stock.
**2** Boil to reduce the sauce to about a quarter of its original quantity. Add the cream and bring to the boil again.
**3** Season to taste with Pernod, pepper and lemon juice and whisk with a mixer until frothy.

## White Butter Sauce

Makes about 250 ml/8 fl oz/1 cup
Preparation time: 40 mins

*1 shallot, finely chopped*

*25 g/1 oz/2 tbsp butter*

*100 ml/3½ fl oz/6½ tbsp dry white wine*

*100 ml/3½ fl oz/6½ tbsp fish stock (see page 17)*

*45 ml/3 tbsp dry vermouth*

*100 ml/3½ fl oz/6½ tbsp single cream*

*50 g/2 oz/¼ cup well chilled butter, cut into small pieces*

*white pepper*

*a few drops of lemon juice*

**1** Fry the chopped shallot in the butter until soft. Pour in the wine, stock and vermouth, bring to the boil and boil steadily to reduce the liquid to about one quarter of its original quantity.
**2** Add the cream and bring to the boil again. Whisk in the butter using an electric whisk.
**3** Season to taste with pepper and lemon juice.

# Crab Sauce

Makes about 750 ml/1¼ pts/3 cups
Preparation time: 80 mins

*500 g/1¼ lb crab shells*

*120 g/4½ oz carrots, finely chopped*

*120 g/4½ oz celery, finely chopped*

*120 g/4½ oz leeks, finely chopped*

*25 g/1 oz/2 tbsp butter*

*500 g/1¼ lb tomatoes, skinned and sieved to purée*

*250 ml/8 fl oz/1 cup dry white wine*

*60 ml/4 tbsp brandy*

*100 ml/6½ tbsp sherry*

*400 ml/14 fl oz/1¾ cups single cream*

*a few drops of lemon juice*

*salt and white pepper*

1 Crush the crab shells up roughly, mix with the vegetables and fry in the butter until the vegetables are soft. 2 Pour in the tomato purée, wine, brandy and sherry, then boil to reduce the liquid almost completely. 3 Add the cream, boil to a creamy consistency and season. 4 Sieve the sauce and re-heat gently.

# Salmon Purée (Quenelle Mixture)

Makes about 450 g/1 lb
Preparation time: 30 mins plus chilling

*225 g/8 oz salmon fillet, skinned and well chilled*

*2 egg whites*

*200 ml/7 fl oz/scant 1 cup double cream, well chilled*

*salt and white pepper*

1 Cut the salmon fillet into cubes.
2 Mix with the egg whites to a fine purée in a food processor or electric blender, then gradually work in the cream. Season to taste with salt and pepper.
3 Finally push the whole mixture through a fine sieve and leave to chill, covered for at least 2 hours.

## Variation

Pike purée can be made in the same way using pike fillet and 300 ml/½ pint/1¼ cups cream. This mixture is used for making pike quenelles.

## Gourmet Tip

Fish purées for Quenelles must always be made with great care, following the recipe exactly. It is essential that all the ingredients have been well chilled before preparation. The cream should always be added slowly, so that the correct quantity is used; this can vary depending on the fish. Before you take the mixture out of the processor, it is always worth cooking one quenelle to test for flavour and consistency. For method, see the recipe for Cream of Parsley Soup with Salmon Quenelles on page 38.

# Cold Fish Dishes

Fish pâté, smoked trout and pickled salmon (Gravad Lax) are all typical examples of classic cold fish dishes. Fish also makes an excellent starter or light evening meal when it is served cold in a salad.

*Pickled Salmon (Gravad Lax), page 22*

# Pickled Salmon (Gravad Lax)

Serves 8 to 10
Preparation time: 1 hour plus marinating
3540 kcal/14810 kJ

| |
|---|
| 1 kg/2 lb salmon |
| 45 ml/3 tbsp salt |
| 2.5 ml/1/2 tbsp black pepper |
| 45 ml/3 tbsp sugar |
| 3 sprigs dill, finely chopped |
| 4 ml/1 tsp juniper berries, crushed |
| 5 ml/1 tsp ground coriander |

**Mustard sauce**

| |
|---|
| 30 ml/2 tbsp Dijon mustard |
| 5 ml/1 tsp German mustard |
| 5 ml/1 tsp white wine vinegar |
| 10 ml/2 tsp caster sugar |
| 1 egg yolk |
| salt and white pepper |
| 100 ml/3 1/2 fl oz/6 1/2 tbsp vegetable oil |
| 45 ml/3 tbsp chopped dill |

1 Fillet the fish, carefully removing the backbone.
2 Mix the salt, pepper, sugar, dill and spices.
3 Spread the mixture over the salmon flesh. Cover with foil and leave in the refrigerator to marinate for about 36 hours, turning frequently.
4 To make the sauce, mix the mustards, vinegar, sugar and egg yolk. Season. Stir in the oil and dill.
5 Slice the salmon thinly and serve with the sauce.

*Photograph page 20*

# Marinated Salmon with Truffle Oil

Serves 4
Preparation time: 15 mins
400 kcal/1675 kJ

| |
|---|
| 225 g/8 oz fresh raw salmon fillet, finely sliced |
| cold-pressed olive oil |
| truffle oil |
| salt and white pepper |
| a few drops of lemon juice |

1 Cut the salmon fillet into wafer-thin slices.
2 Pour a little olive oil and truffle oil on to 4 chilled plates and sprinkle with salt and pepper.
3 Place the salmon slices on the plate and season again lightly. Dot with oil and lemon juice and serve immediately.

> **Gourmet Tip**
> Truffle oil is olive oil flavoured with white truffles. Truffles have a very strong flavour and should be mixed in a ratio of 1 part truffle to 5 parts olive oil.
> Instead of truffle oil, you could use white truffles. These can be sprinkled over the salmon using a special grater.

*Photograph opposite (top)*

# Salmon and Herring Tartar

Serves 4
Preparation time: 25 mins
1900 kcal/7950 kJ

| |
|---|
| 8 small slices white bread |
| 50 g/2 oz/1/3 cup butter |
| 225 g/8 oz fresh salmon fillet |
| salt and white pepper |
| a few drops of lemon juice |
| olive oil |
| 225 g/4 oz filleted salt herring |
| 1 shallot, finely chopped |
| 1/4 cucumber, thinly sliced |
| 1 tomato, thinly sliced |
| 25 g/1 oz capers |
| 25 g/1 oz salmon caviar or lumpfish caviar |

1 Fry the slices of bread in the butter until golden on both sides.
2 Chop the salmon fillet finely and season with salt, pepper, lemon juice and olive oil.
3 Chop and season the herring fillet with pepper, lemon juice, olive oil and chopped shallot.
4 Arrange the cucumber slices on one half of the bread and the tomato slices on the other.
5 Serve the herring tartar on the tomato and the salmon tartar on the cucumber.
6 Garnish the herrings with capers and the salmon with caviar.

*Photograph opposite (bottom)*

23

# Haddock Salad Julienne

Serves 4
Preparation time: 50 mins
1680 kcal/7030 kJ

| |
|---|
| *400 g/4 oz haddock fillet* |
| *1 l/1³/4 pts/4¹/4 cups court bouillon (see page 18)* |
| *100 g/4 oz celery* |
| *100 g/4 oz young carrots* |
| *100 g/4 oz kohlrabi* |
| *100 g/4 oz young peas* |
| *5 ml/1 tsp Dijon mustard* |
| *5 ml/1 tsp caster sugar* |
| *30 ml/2 tbsp white wine vinegar* |
| *30 ml/2 tbsp dry white wine* |
| *150 ml/¹/4 pt/²/3 cup salad oil* |
| *salt and white pepper* |
| *4 lettuce leaves* |

1 Wash the haddock fillet and poach it in the simmering court bouillon for 10 to 15 minutes.

2 Cut the vegetables into matchstick-sized strips and boil, with the peas, in salted water until they are just tender. Cool them quickly with iced water and drain.

3 Make the vinaigrette by mixing the mustard, sugar, wine vinegar, wine, oil, salt and pepper.

4 Break the haddock up into large chunks and carefully mix together with the vegetables.

5 Serve on individual plates. Pile the fish and vegetables on to the lettuce leaves and pour over the vinaigrette.

*Photograph (bottom)*

24

# Plaice Fillet with Tomatoes and Basil

Serves 4
Preparation time: 30 mins
700 kcal/2930 kJ

| |
|---|
| 4 large tomatoes, thinly sliced |
| salt and white pepper |
| red wine vinegar |
| 4 x 120 g/4 ½ oz plaice fillets |
| olive oil |
| a few fresh basil leaves, cut into strips |
| 1 lemon, cut into quarters |

**1** Arrange the sliced tomatoes on 4 plates. Season lightly with salt and pepper and coat with a little red wine vinegar.
**2** Brush the flesh sides of the fish with oil then sprinkle with salt. Brown under the grill for a few minutes on each side.
**3** Serve the fish hot on the bed of tomato slices, sprinkled with the basil.
**4** Pass some lemon quarters and extra oil around separately.

*Photograph (top)*

## Trout with Horseradish Sauce

Serves 4
Preparation time: 45 mins
850 kcal/3560 kJ

| |
|---|
| 2 x 300 g/11 oz trout |
| 1 l/1³/₄ pts/4¹/₄ cups court bouillon (see page 18) |
| 2 bunches watercress |
| 60 ml/4 tbsp creme fraîche |
| 30 ml/2 tbsp mayonnaise |
| 15 ml/1 tbsp freshly grated horseradish |
| 15 ml/1 tbsp finely chopped dill |
| salt and white pepper |
| a few drops of lemon juice |

1 Place the trout in the hot but not boiling court bouillon and poach on a low heat for about 10 minutes. Leave to cool.
2 Wash the watercress and pat dry.
3 To make the sauce, stir together the creme fraîche, mayonnaise, horseradish and dill, and season to taste with salt, pepper and lemon juice.
4 Remove the fish from the court bouillon and drain off any excess liquid. Skin the fish by running a small knife down the backbone, starting at the head.
5 Next fillet the fish with the help of a fork and spoon. Starting at the head again, release the upper fillet and finally remove the bones from the tail end to release the lower fillet.
6 Arrange the trout fillets with the watercress and coat with some of the sauce. Serve the rest of the sauce separately.

**Note**
The trout should be as fresh as possible and preferably be killed less than 12 hours before required. Otherwise it may break up whilst poaching.

*Photograph opposite (top).*

## Fish Fillet with Herb Sauce

Serves 4
Preparation time: 45 mins
1900 kcal/7950 kJ

| |
|---|
| 450 g/1 lb white fish fillet (whiting, haddock or plaice) |
| salt |
| a few drops of lemon juice |
| 45 ml/3 tbsp cold-pressed olive oil |
| 15 ml/1 tbsp white wine vinegar |
| pepper |
| 1 head frisée lettuce |
| 2 cartons cress |
| **Herb sauce:** |
| 5 ml/1 tsp French mustard |
| 30 ml/2 tbsp fish stock |
| 10 ml/2 tbsp dry vermouth |
| a pinch of sugar |
| salt and pepper |
| 50 g/2 oz fresh herbs (parsley, dill, chervil, tarragon) |
| 60 ml/4 tbsp creme fraîche |

1 Cut up the fish into portions and season lightly with salt and lemon juice.
2 Make the vinaigrette by mixing together 30 ml/2 tbsp olive oil and 30 ml/2 tbsp white wine vinegar and seasoning with salt and pepper.
3 Wash the frisée lettuce and the cress and pat dry.
4 To make the herb sauce, purée together the mustard, fish stock, vermouth, seasonings and herbs in a food processor or electric blender. Finally add the creme fraîche and adjust the seasoning to taste.
5 Trickle the remaining oil over the fish fillets and brown under the grill on both sides.
6 Mix the vinaigrette with the lettuce and arrange on 4 plates. Add the fish and finally pour over the herb sauce.

*Photograph opposite (bottom)*

# Brill and Bean Slice

Serves 10
Preparation time: 90 mins
plus setting
1250 kcal/5230 kJ

*2 envelopes powdered gelatine*

*600 ml/1 pt/2¹/₂ cups fish stock (see page 17)*

*150 ml/¹/₄ pt/²/₃ cup Riesling, medium dry*

*salt and pepper*

*450 g/1 lb fillet brill or lemon sole*

*225 g/8 oz French beans*

*225 g/8 oz tomatoes*

*a few basil leaves, cut into strips*

**1** Soften the gelatine in a few tablespoons of cold water. Pour into pan and melt gently over a low heat.
**2** Heat the clear fish stock (preferably made with the head and bones of the brill) together with the wine and season to taste with salt and pepper.
**3** Add the fish to the stock and leave to stand for about 5 minutes. Remove and leave to cool.
**4** Stir the gelatine into the hot stock then pass the liquid through a sieve.
**5** Wash the beans and cook in boiling salted water for about 5 minutes until just tender. Rinse with iced water.
**6** Immerse the tomatoes in boiling water for 10 seconds and rinse with cold water. Peel, seed and chop up the flesh.

**7** The fish jelly should have cooled by now. Pour it into a 1 l/1³/₄ pt/4¹/₄ cup mould and place it in iced water for a few minutes. A thin layer of jelly should set around the edges. Pour out the remaining liquid and keep it to one side.
**8** Arrange the fine beans closely together along the base of the mould. Place half the fish on top, followed by the tomatoes and basil, the rest of the fish and finally the second half of the beans. Fill the mould up with the rest of the jelly and refrigerate overnight.
**9** Turn out the mould and cut the jelly into slices. Serve garnished with salad.

# Red Mullet with Asparagus

Serves 4
Preparation time: 40 mins
1950 kcal/8160 kJ

---

450 g/1 *lb* asparagus tips

1 frisée lettuce

salt and white pepper

30 ml/2 *tbsp* white wine vinegar

60 ml/¼ *tbsp* sunflower oil

15 ml/1 *tbsp* walnut oil

4 x 100 g/4 *oz* red mullet fillets

40 g/1½ *oz* pine nuts, toasted until golden

---

1 Peel, wash and cook the asparagus in boiling salted water until just tender. Cool in iced water and pat dry.
2 Wash the frisée lettuce and pat dry.
3 Mix some salt and pepper with the wine vinegar until absorbed, then stir in the sunflower and walnut oils.
4 Season the fish lightly and shallow fry in a little oil on both sides for about 2 minutes.
5 Mix the frisée lettuce and the asparagus with the dressing and arrange on 4 plates. Place the warm red mullet fillets on top and sprinkle with pine nuts.

**Variation**
Other suitable fish for this recipe are gurnard, redfish or sea bass.

*Photograph opposite (top)*

# Monkfish with Oak-Leaf Salad

Serves 4
Preparation time: 50 mins
1900 kcal/7950 kJ

---

1 oak-leaf lettuce

750 g/1¾ *lb* monkfish

salt and white pepper

15 ml/1 *tbsp* sherry vinegar

15 ml/1 *tbsp* red wine vinegar

75 ml/5 *tbsp* olive oil

225 g/8 *oz* mushrooms, sliced

a few sprigs of chervil

---

1 Wash and pat the lettuce dry.
2 Skin the monkfish with a small, sharp knife and cut the fish into 12 equal slices.
3 To make the vinaigrette, mix together the salt, pepper, vinegars and oil.
4 Toss the sliced mushrooms with a little of the vinaigrette.
5 Shallow fry the monkfish on both sides in a little extra oil and salt lightly.
6 Divide the oak-leaf lettuce between the plates and pour a little of the vinaigrette over each. Arrange the mushrooms and the fish on top. Garnish with fresh chervil.

**Variation**
Other suitable fish for this recipe are cod and halibut.

*Photograph opposite (centre)*

# Smoked Trout Chanterelle

Serves 4
Preparation time: 45 mins
1850 kcal/7740 kJ

---

100 g/4 *oz* fresh spinach leaves

2 smoked trout

1 shallot, finely chopped

60 ml/4 *tbsp* olive oil

225 g/8 *oz* fresh chanterelle mushrooms

salt and white pepper

30 ml/2 *tbsp* white wine vinegar

30 ml/2 *tbsp* walnut oil

a few sprigs of chervil

---

1 Wash the spinach and dry on kitchen paper.
2 Fillet the trout.
3 Fry the shallot gently in the 30 ml/2 tbsp olive oil, wash the mushrooms and add them to the pan. Season to taste with salt and pepper and allow to cook for a few minutes.
4 To make the vinaigrette, beat some salt and pepper with the wine vinegar until it has dissolved. Stir in rest of the olive oil and the walnut oil.
5 Arrange the spinach leaves on the plates and trickle some of the vinaigrette over each.
6 Slice the trout fillets diagonally and arrange on top of the spinach. Add the chanterelle mushrooms and garnish with fresh chervil.

*Photograph opposite (bottom)*

# Salmon and Pike Terrine

Serves 10
Preparation time: 1¼ hours
2900 kcal/12135 kJ

---

*100 g/4 oz broccoli florets*

*225 g/8 oz salmon fillet*

*a few drops of lemon juice*

*salt*

*10 ml/2 tsp brandy*

*450 g/1 lb salmon purée (see page 19)*

*15 ml/1 tbsp finely chopped dill*

*450 g/1 lb pike purée (see page 19)*

1 Blanch the broccoli in boiling salted water and cool off at once in iced water. Thoroughly pat dry.
2 Cut up the salmon into large chunks and marinate in lemon juice, salt and brandy for about 1 hour.
3 Line a mould with foil, allowing an overlap of about 10 cm/4 in.
4 Using a piping bag, cover the base and sides of the mould with half the salmon purée.
5 Mix the chunks of salmon, broccoli, dill and pike purée well together. Press this mixture into the mould and cover with the remaining salmon purée.
6 Cover the terrine tightly with the rest of the foil and stand the mould in a baking dish filled with 2 cm/¾ in lukewarm water. Bake for 50 minutes in an oven pre-heated to 150°C/300°F/gas mark 2.
7 Leave the terrine to cool overnight in the mould and then remove and cut into 1 cm/½ in slices.

---

**Gourmet Tip**
Garnish the terrine with a salad and serve with creme fraîche and fresh herbs.

# Smoked Trout Mousse

Serves 4
Preparation time: 60 mins
plus chilling
1500 kcal/6275 kJ

---

1 envelope gelatine

50 ml/2 fl oz/¹/₄ cup sweet white wine

225 g/8 oz trout, filleted

a few drops of lemon juice

salt and cayenne pepper

250 ml/8 fl oz/1 cup whipping cream, whipped

a few sprigs of dill

60 ml/4 tbsp creme fraîche

pepper

---

1 Soften the gelatine in 30 ml/2 tbsp cold water, then stir over low heat until melted. Heat the wine and add to the gelatine.
2 Blend the filleted trout and gelatine mixture to a purée, then rub through a fine sieve. Season to taste with lemon juice, salt and a little cayenne pepper.
3 Carefully mix in a third of the whipped cream and gradually add the rest.
4 Pipe the mousse into 4 glasses.
5 Wash the dill, reserving a few sprigs for decoration and chop the rest.
6 Mix the creme fraîche with the dill and season to taste with salt, lemon juice and pepper.
7 When the mousse has set, serve with the creme fraîche and dill.

*Photograph opposite (top).*

# Sole with Mange-Tout

Serves 4
Preparation time: 60 mins
1180 kcal/4940 kJ

---

350 g/12 oz mange-tout

15 ml/1 tbsp white wine vinegar

15 ml/1 tbsp balsamic vinegar

salt and cayenne pepper

a pinch of sugar

60 ml/4 tbsp olive or corn oil

1 shallot, finely chopped

4 x 75 g/3 oz sole fillets

a few drops of lemon juice

a few basil leaves

---

1 Wash the mange-tout and blanch in boiling salted water for 2 to 4 minutes. Rinse in iced water and leave to dry on a towel.
2 Stir together the wine and balsamic vinegars, salt, cayenne pepper and sugar and whisk in the olive oil. Add the shallot.
3 Season the sole fillets with salt and a few drops of lemon juice. Brush with extra oil and cook under a hot grill for about 3 minutes on each side.
4 Arrange the mange-tout in the form of a flower on 4 plates. Place the sole fillets in the centre and dribble the vinaigrette over. Garnish with basil leaves.

*Photograph opposite (bottom left).*

# Turbot with Asparagus Spears

Serves 4
Preparation time: 50 mins
1350 kcal/5650 kJ

---

225 g/8 oz asparagus spears

8 shallots, finely chopped

a pinch of sugar

100 ml/3¹/₂ fl oz/6¹/₂ tbsp red wine

30 ml/2 tbsp salted butter

30 ml/2 tbsp balsamic vinegar

450 g/1 lb turbot or sole fillets

15 ml/1 tbsp lemon juice

salt and pepper

15 ml/1 tbsp olive oil

---

1 Wash the asparagus and blanch for a few minutes in boiling water without salt. Cool off immediately with iced water and leave to dry.
2 Bring the shallots to the boil with the sugar and red wine. Swirl in the salted butter and season with a little balsamic vinegar.
3 Poach the turbot fillets for about 7 minutes in just enough lightly salted water to cover.
4 Mix together the lemon juice, pepper, salt and olive oil. Coat the asparagus in the marinade then arrange it on individual plates. Put the lukewarm turbot fillets on top and coat with the red wine and shallot mixture.

*Photograph opposite (bottom right)*

# Soups and Light Fish Dishes

Tasty fish soups are usually amongst the regional specialities of coastal areas. There are many mouthwatering varieties of soup as well as other fish delicacies. A selection of these is given in this section.

*Mediterranean Fish Soup, page 38*

# Mediterranean Fish Soup

Serves 4
Preparation time: 40 mins
1500 kcal/6275 kJ

| |
|---|
| 1 kg/2 lb Mediterranean fish |
| (red mullet, whiting or redfish) |
| 50 g/2 oz leeks, cut into strips |
| 50 g/2 oz carrots, cut into strips |
| 50 g/2 oz celery, cut into strips |
| 6 saffron strands |
| 60 ml/4 tbsp olive or corn oil |
| 750 ml/1 1/4 pts clear fish stock, preferably made from flat fish (see page 17) |
| salt |
| white pepper |
| a few drops of Pernod |

1 Fillet the fish carefully, rinse in cold water and leave to dry on kitchen paper.
2 Brown the vegetables and the saffron in hot oil for a few minutes and add the fish stock. Bring to the boil and season to taste with salt and pepper.
3 Add the fish fillets to the soup and leave to stand for about 5 minutes until cooked through. Flavour with a little Pernod.
4 Place about half a fillet of each different kind of fish on warmed soup dishes and add the soup and vegetables.

*Photograph page 36*

# Cream of Tomato Soup with Sole

Serves 4
Preparation time: 30 mins
2360 kcal/9880 kJ

| |
|---|
| 4 shallots, finely chopped |
| 60 ml/4 tbsp butter |
| 225 g/8 oz peeled tomatoes, diced |
| 250 ml/8 fl oz/1 cup fish stock (see page 17) |
| salt |
| a pinch of sugar |
| cayenne pepper |
| a few drops of lemon juice |
| 400 ml/14 fl oz/1 3/4 cups single cream |
| 450 g/1 lb sole fillets |
| a few basil leaves, cut into strips |

1 Fry the shallots in the butter until softened. Add the tomatoes and fish stock and season to taste with the salt, sugar, cayenne and lemon juice.
2 Bring to the boil and simmer for 10 minutes before adding the cream. Season again if necessary and purée in an electric blender or food processor. Pass through a sieve and return to the pan.
3 Cut the sole fillets into 5 mm/1/4 in strips and simmer in the hot soup for about 2 minutes until cooked.
4 Finally stir in the basil leaves and serve the soup in warmed soup dishes.

*Photograph opposite (top)*

# Parsley Soup with Salmon Quenelles

Serves 4
Preparation time: 40 mins
1980 kcal/8285 kJ

| |
|---|
| 15 ml/1 tbsp butter |
| 2 shallots, finely chopped |
| 30 ml/2 tbsp dry vermouth |
| 450 ml/3/4 pt/2 cups fish stock (see page 17) |
| 450 ml/3/4 pt/2 cups single cream |
| salt |
| cayenne pepper |
| 225 g/8 oz salmon purée (see page 19) |
| 1 bunch parsley, finely chopped |
| 30 ml/2 tbsp salted butter |

1 Melt the butter, add the shallots and fry until softened. Pour in the fish stock and vermouth, bring to the boil and simmer for 5 minutes. Add the cream and season to taste with salt and cayenne pepper.
2 Using a teaspoon, make small quenelles from the salmon purée and leave these to stand in barely simmering salted water for 5 minutes.
3 Purée the soup with the chopped parsley and salted butter. Serve in warmed soup dishes with the salmon quenelles.
**Variation**
Instead of salmon quenelles you could use thin slices of poached eel.

*Photograph opposite (bottom)*

# Vegetable Soup with Fillet of Gurnard

Serves 4
Preparation time: 35 mins
1250 kcal/5235 kJ

| |
|---|
| 100 g/*4 oz* carrots, cut into strips |
| 100 g/*4 oz* kohlrabi, cut into strips |
| 15 g/*¹/₂ oz*/1 tbsp butter |
| 45 ml/*3 tbsp* dry vermouth |
| 90 ml/*6 tbsp* dry white wine |
| 750 ml/1 ¹/₄ *pts*/3 cups clear fish stock (see page 17) |
| 4 x 75 g/*3 oz* gurnard fillets |
| 100 g/*4 oz* spring peas |
| salt |
| pepper |

**1** Fry the carrots and kohlrabi strips in the butter until softened. Pour in the vermouth and wine and boil to reduce the liquid until only a few tablespoons remain.
**2** Add the fish stock and reheat. Cut each gurnard fillet in half and add to the soup with the peas. Bring to the boil and simmer gently for 2 minutes.
**3** Season to taste with salt and pepper and serve in warmed soup dishes.

**Variation**
Instead of gurnard fillets, the fish can be served with pike quenelles and fresh, finely chopped dill.

*Photograph (left)*

# Salmon with Vegetable Consommé

Serves 4
Preparation time: 35 mins
1080 kcal/4520 kJ

| |
|---|
| *50 g/2 oz leeks, cut into strips* |
| *50 g/2 oz carrots, cut into strips* |
| *50 g/2 oz celery, cut into strips* |
| *30 ml/2 tbsp olive oil* |
| *salt and pepper* |
| *a few strands of saffron* |
| *45 ml/3 tbsp dry vermouth* |
| *750 ml/1 1/4 pts/3 cups clear, strong fish stock (page 17)* |
| *225 g/8 oz salmon fillet* |
| *a few drops of lemon juice* |

**1** Fry the vegetables in the olive oil until softened, then season lightly with salt and pepper and add the saffron strands.
**2** Add the vermouth and boil until the liquid has reduced almost completely. Pour in the fish stock and bring back to the boil.
**3** Cut the salmon fillet into thick strips, add to the soup and simmer gently for about 30 seconds.
**4** Season the soup again with salt, pepper and lemon juice and serve straight away in warmed soup dishes.
**Variation**
River trout and salmon trout are also suitable for this recipe.

*Photograph (right)*

## Puff Pastry Soup Surprise

Serves 4
Preparation time: 90 mins
2350 kcal/9830 kJ

| |
|---|
| 2 shallots, finely chopped |
| 25 g/1 oz leek, cut into strips |
| 25 g/1 oz carrot, cut into strips |
| 25 g/1 oz celery, cut into strips |
| 25 g/1 oz/2 tbsp butter |
| 45 ml/3 tbsp dry vermouth |
| 750 ml/1¹/₄ pts/3 cups clear, strong fish stock, preferably made from flat fish (see page 17) |
| salt |
| cayenne pepper |
| 225 g/8 oz cod fillet |
| 4 x 225 g/8 oz plaice fillets |
| 400 g/14 oz puff pastry (frozen) |
| 2 egg yolks |
| 20 ml/2 tbsp water |

1 Fry the shallots with the vegetables in the butter until softened. Add the vermouth and boil to reduce the liquid almost completely.
2 Add the fish stock, bring to the boil and season to taste with salt and cayenne pepper. Remove from the heat and allow to cool.
3 Cut the cod fillet into 4 slices and divide the cod and plaice between 4 deep ovenproof soup bowls. Pour the cooled fish soup into each bowl up to 2 cm/³/₄ in below the rim.
4 Roll out the puff pastry to about 4 mm/¹/₄ in thick. Cut out 4 pieces of pastry to overlap the soup bowls by 2.5 cm/1 in around the edges.
5 Beat the egg yolks with the water and brush over the edge of the pastry and the rims of the soup bowls. Place the pastry tops over each filled soup bowl and press the edges together firmly.
6 Brush the puff pastry with the egg yolk and water and bake for about 15 minutes in a pre-heated oven at 200°C/400°F/gas mark 6 until golden brown. Serve at once.

### Variation
Other suitable fish include freshwater fish such as trout, perch or catfish.

*Photograph opposite (top)*

## Matelote of Freshwater Fish

Serves 4
Preparation time: 50 mins
2360 kcal/9875 kJ

| |
|---|
| 100 g/4 oz smoked bacon |
| 75 g/3 oz/¹/₃ cup butter |
| 50 g/2 oz leeks, cut into strips |
| 50 g/2 oz carrots, cut into strips |
| 50 g/2 oz celery, cut into strips |
| 2 cloves garlic, crushed |
| 20 shallots |
| 100 g/4 oz mushrooms, sliced |
| 1 sprig thyme |
| 1 bay leaf |
| 2 sprigs parsley |
| 750 ml/1¹/₄ pts/3 cups red wine |
| salt |
| pepper |
| 1 kg/2 lb freshwater fish (eel, tench or carp) |

1 Dice the bacon finely and fry in two-thirds of the butter with the vegetables, crushed garlic cloves, whole peeled shallots, mushrooms and herbs.
2 Pour in the red wine and boil to reduce the liquid to about two-thirds of the original quantity. Season lightly with a little salt and pepper.
3 Wash the fish, remove the heads and cut the flesh into pieces.
4 Heat the remaining butter in a frying pan and fry the fish pieces over a low heat.
5 Add the fish pieces to the vegetables and wine, leave to stand for about 5 minutes and season again if necessary. Serve with slices of white bread fried in butter.

*Photograph opposite (bottom)*

43

# Pike Quenelles with Crab Sauce

Serves 4
Preparation time: 45 mins
2050 kcal/8580 kJ

| |
|---|
| *450 g/1 lb fresh spinach* |
| *salt* |
| *1 l/1³/₄ **pts**/4¹/₄ cups fish stock (see page 17)* |
| *450 g/1 lb pike purée (see page 19)* |
| *750 ml/1¹/₄ **pts**/3 cups crab sauce (see page 19)* |
| *15 ml/1 **tbsp** butter* |
| *white pepper* |
| *90 ml/**6 tbsp** cream, whipped* |
| *20 ml/**4 tsp** grated Parmesan cheese* |

1 Wash the spinach and blanch it in boiling, salted water. Cool off immediately in iced water and leave to drain in a sieve.
2 Heat up the fish stock. Using a dessert spoon, make small quenelles from the pike purée and simmer these very gently for about 10 minutes in the fish stock.
3 Heat up the crab sauce and season if necessary. Swirl in the butter and season to taste with pepper.
4 Divide the spinach between flameproof soup dishes, arrange the quenelles on top and pour the crab sauce over them.
5 Coat with the cream, sprinkle with Parmesan cheese and brown under the grill.

*Photograph (left)*

# Salmon Timbale

Serves 4
Preparation time: 45 mins
2350 kcal/9830 kJ

---

*450 g/1 lb salmon purée
(see page 19)*

*1 shallot, finely chopped*

*50 g/2 oz/¹/₄ cup butter*

*100 ml/3¹/₂ fl oz/6¹/₂ tbsp
dry white wine*

*100 ml/3¹/₂ fl oz/6¹/₂ tbsp
dry vermouth*

*100 ml/3¹/₂ fl oz/6¹/₂ tbsp
fish stock (see page 17)*

*45 ml/3 tbsp cream*

*2 bunches mixed herbs*

*a handful of fresh spinach*

*a few drops of lemon juice*

*salt and white pepper*

---

**1** Chill the salmon purée and use to fill 4 buttered moulds. Cover with buttered foil and stand them in a baking dish filled with 2 cm/³/₄ in lukewarm water. Bake in a pre-heated oven at 180°C/350°F/gas mark 4 for 20 minutes.
**2** Fry the shallot in butter until soft, add the wine, vermouth and stock and boil down almost completely.
**3** Add the cream and bring back to the boil. Add remaining butter, the herbs and spinach and blend to a fine purée.
**4** Season the sauce to taste with the lemon juice, salt and pepper.
**5** Divide the sauce between warmed soup bowls and turn out the salmon timbales on top.

*Photograph (right)*

45

# Salmon Pasta Mozzarella

Serves 4
Preparation time: 30 mins
2200 kcal/9210 kJ

| |
|---|
| *225 g/8 oz tagliatelle* |
| *salt* |
| *225 g/8 oz salmon fillet* |
| *150 g/15 oz mozzarella cheese* |
| *2 tomatoes, de-seeded and diced* |
| *a few basil leaves, cut into strips* |
| *30 ml/2 tbsp olive oil* |
| *salt and white pepper* |
| *60 ml/4 tbsp creme fraîche* |

1 Boil the tagliatelle in salted water until *al dente*.
2 Dice the salmon fillet and mozzarella cheese. Mix the salmon, mozzarella, tomatoes, basil and olive oil together with the boiling hot pasta. Season to taste with salt and pepper.
3 Pile the mixture into a pie dish, pour the creme fraîche over the top and flash bake in an oven pre-heated to 230°C/450°F/gas mark 8 for 2 to 2½ minutes until the cheese just starts to melt. Serve immediately.
**Variation**
Cod fillet is also suitable for this recipe.

*Photograph opposite (bottom)*

# Pike and Salmon Pasta Parcels

Serves 4
Preparation time: 70 mins
1430 kcal/5990 kJ

| |
|---|
| **Dough** |
| *8 ml/¹/₂ tbsp olive oil* |
| *a pinch salt* |
| *2 eggs* |
| *200 g/7 oz/scant 1 cup flour* |
| **Filling** |
| *65 g/2¹/₂ oz salmon fillet* |
| *a little dill, finely chopped* |
| *100 g/4 oz pike purée (see page 19)* |
| *salt* |
| *pepper* |
| *1 egg, beaten* |

1 To make the dough, mix together the oil, salt and eggs. Sieve the flour and gradually work it into the egg and oil mixture. Knead the dough by hand until it is smooth. Cover with a cloth and leave for 1 hour.
2 Chop the salmon fillet coarsely and mix with the dill and pike purée to make filling. Season to taste with salt and pepper.
3 Divide the dough into 2 halves and roll out thinly on a floured surface. Mark out squares about 2.5 cm/1 in wide with the back of a knife on one half of the dough. Brush with beaten egg.
4 Place a teaspoon of filling in the centre of each square. Lay the second half of the dough on top and press down around the filling with your fingers, trying to avoid any air pockets. Cut the pasta parcels out with a pastry cutter.
5 Cook the pasta parcels in boiling salted water for about 5 minutes, testing them after 4 minutes.
6 Remove with a slatted spoon and allow to drain well before serving hot.

*Photograph opposite (top)*

---

**Gourmet Tip**
These pasta parcels taste very good with White Butter Sauce (see page 18) and a little dill.

---

# Hot Fish Dishes

Nowadays there are so many different ways of cooking fish: it can be poached, grilled, baked or fried in its own juices and served with a wide variety of sauces. The following chapter shows how to prepare a selection of both traditional and more unusual fine fish dishes.

*Sea Bass in Salt Pastry,*
*page 50*

# Sea Bass Baked in Salt Pastry

Serves 4
Preparation time: 90 mins
plus chilling
2040 kcal/8540 kJ

**Pastry**
500 g/1 ¼ lb/2 ¼ cups plain flour

300 g/11 oz salt

2 eggs

300 ml/½ pint/1 ¼ cups water

**Fish**
1 x 1.5 kg (3½ lb) sea bass

salt

white pepper

a little parsley and tarragon

1 small sprig rosemary

1 egg, beaten

1 onion, finely chopped

50 g/2 oz/¼ cup butter

100 ml/3½ fl oz/6½ tbsp dry white wine

10 ml/2 tbsp fish stock

45 ml/3 tbsp dry vermouth

100 ml/3½ fl oz/6½ tbsp single cream

1 bunch chives, finely chopped

1 Knead together the pastry ingredients and leave to chill in the refrigerator for 2 hours.
2 Remove the scales from the fish and gut. Rinse under cold water, pat dry, season with salt and pepper and fill with the fresh herbs.
3 Roll out the salt pastry to about 1 cm/½ in thick and wrap it around the fish. Brush beaten egg along the edges and press together well. Brush beaten egg over all the pastry.
4 Bake the fish in a pre-heated oven at 200°C/400°F/gas mark 6 for 20 to 25 minutes.
5 Fry the onion in half the butter until soft. Pour in the wine, fish stock and vermouth and boil to reduce the liquid almost completely.
6 Add the cream and bring back to the boil, then add the remaining butter and mix to a purée in an electric blender. Stir in the chives and season with salt and pepper.
7 Remove the fish from the oven and cut off the salt pastry surround.
8 Take out the fish fillets with a spoon and fork and serve with the chive sauce on warmed plates. The salt pastry protects the fish during cooking and should not be eaten.

*Photograph page 48*

# Crispy Topped Carp

Serves 4
Preparation time: 80 mins
2500 kcal/10465 kJ

2 x 1 kg/2 lb carp

salt

a few drops of lemon juice

75 g/3 oz/⅓ cup butter

250 ml/8 fl oz/1 cup fish stock (see page 17)

2 sprigs parsley

2 sprigs dill

200 ml/7 fl oz/scant 1 cup single cream

25 g/1 oz/½ cup fresh white breadcrumbs

1 Wash the carp then sprinkle with salt and lemon juice. Fry lightly on both sides in 50 g/2 oz/¼ cup butter over a low heat.
2 Place in an ovenproof dish, pour over the fish stock, add the herbs and cover well with aluminium foil.
3 Bake in a pre-heated oven at 200°C/400°F/gas mark 6 for about 20 minutes.
4 Remove the foil, turn the fish round and pour over the cream. Sprinkle with breadcrumbs and place knobs of the remaining butter on top.
5 Return to the oven uncovered and bake for a further 20 minutes until the breadcrumbs are lightly browned.
6 Remove the fish with a slotted spoon and keep warm. Boil the sauce down until it thickens, season to taste, pass through a sieve, reheat and serve separately with the fish.
**Variation**
Cod is also suitable for this dish.

*Photograph opposite*

51

# John Dory with Brandied Crab Sauce

Serves 4
Preparation time: 40 mins
1800 kcal/7535 kJ

| |
|---|
| *2 leeks, cut into strips* |
| *25 g/1 oz/2 tbsp butter* |
| *salt* |
| *4 John Dory fillets* |
| *a few drops of lemon juice* |
| *15 ml/1 tbsp olive oil* |
| *400 ml/14 fl oz/1³/₄ cups crab sauce (see page 19)* |
| *a few drops of brandy* |
| *a few basil leaves* |

**1** Fry the leeks gently in 1 tbsp butter until softened, salt lightly and continue to cook the leeks in their own juices.
**2** Lightly salt the fish fillets and sprinkle with lemon juice. Heat the remaining butter and the olive oil in a frying pan and cook the fillets over a low heat for about 4 minutes, depending on the thickness of the fish. Turn once.
**3** Heat up the crab sauce and season with a few drops of brandy.
**4** Arrange the leek strips in the middle of the plates, place the fish on top and coat with the crab sauce.
**5** Garnish with fresh basil leaves.

*Photograph (top)*

# Catfish Julienne

Serves 4
Preparation time: 45 mins
2080 kcal/8710 kJ

---

*750 g/1³/₄ lb catfish (or whiting), cut into slices*

---

*salt*

---

*a few drops of lemon juice*

---

*100 g/4 oz carrots, cut into strips*

---

*100 g/4 oz celery, cut into strips*

---

*100 g/4 oz leeks, cut into strips*

---

*75 g/3 oz/¹/₃ cup butter*

---

*45 ml/3 tbsp dry vermouth*

---

*45 ml/3 tbsp dry white wine*

---

*45 ml/3 tbsp fish stock (see page 17)*

---

*white pepper*

---

**1** Wash the fish and season with salt and lemon juice.
**2** Fry the vegetables in the butter in a covered pan until softened, then add the vermouth, wine and fish stock.
**3** Place the fish in the pan, cover and poach on a low heat for about 15 minutes.
**4** Season with a little pepper and serve in warmed soup dishes.

*Photograph (bottom)*

## Slash-Grilled Mackerel with Tomato

Serves 4
Preparation time: 30 mins
2150 kcal/9000 kJ

4 x 350 g *(12 oz)* mackerel
a few drops of lemon juice
salt and pepper
150 ml/*¹/₄ pint/²/₃ cup* olive or corn oil
30 ml/*2 tbsp* red wine vinegar
2 beef tomatoes
a few basil leaves, cut into strips

1 Gut the mackerel, wash and pat dry. Season inside and out with salt, pepper and lemon juice.
2 Using a sharp knife, make deep cuts along the back of the fish at intervals of about 1 cm/¹/₂ in. This will ensure that the fish cooks evenly.
3 Brush 60 ml/4 tbsp oil over the fish and grill on both sides under a low heat for about 10 minutes.
4 To make the vinaigrette, season the red wine vinegar to taste with salt and pepper, then mix in the remaining oil.
5 Skin the tomatoes, quarter, seed and cut into small cubes. Mix together with the vinaigrette and basil leaves and serve with the grilled fish.

*Photograph opposite (top)*

## Golden Trout with Almonds

Serves 4
Preparation time: 50 mins
1900 kcal/7955 kJ

4 x 225 g/*8 oz* trout
salt
a few drops of lemon juice
30 ml/*2 tbsp* plain flour
75 g/*3 oz*/*¹/₃ cup* butter
50 g/*2 oz*/*¹/₄ cup* flaked almonds
2 sprigs parsley, finely chopped

1 Clean the trout thoroughly and season with salt and lemon juice.
2 Dip into the flour and fry in two-thirds of the hot melted butter for about 10 minutes until golden brown on both sides. Cover the pan so they cook evenly.
3 Place the trout on warmed plates.
4 Heat the rest of the butter in a clean frying pan, add the almonds and cook until they turn golden brown. Sprinkle over the fish and garnish with a little parsley.

*Photograph opposite (centre)*

## Perch Fillets with Smoked Rashers

Serves 4
Preparation time: 35 mins
1900 kcal/7955 kJ

4 x 225 g/*8 oz* perch fillets
salt
a few drops of lemon juice
30 ml/*2 tbsp* plain flour
75 g/*3 oz*/*¹/₃ cup* butter, melted
8 rashers smoked bacon
1 bunch chervil

1 Cut off any remaining fins and skin from the perch, rinse under cold water and pat dry.
2 Season the fillets with salt and lemon juice, then dust with flour.
3 Heat up two-thirds of the butter in a heavy frying pan. Fry the perch fillets until they are golden brown on both sides. Remove them from the pan and keep them warm.
4 Fry the bacon in a non-stick pan without extra fat until crispy.
5 Arrange the perch on warmed plates and place the bacon on top.
6 Dribble a little melted butter over and garnish with fresh chervil.
**Variation**
Trout is also suitable for this recipe.

*Photograph opposite (bottom)*

# Gold Bream with Vegetables

Serves 4
Preparation time: 35 mins
1950 kcal/8160 kJ

---

*2 x 500 g (1 1/4 lb) gold bream, scaled and filleted*

---

*salt*

---

*flour for dusting*

---

*15 ml/1 **tbsp** butter*

---

*15 ml/1 **tbsp** olive oil*

---

*100 g/4 **oz** celery, cut into strips*

---

*100 g/4 **oz** carrots, cut into strips*

---

*225 g/8 **oz** mange-tout*

---

*100 ml/3 1/2 **fl oz**/6 1/2 tbsp fish stock (see page 17)*

---

*45 ml/3 **tbsp** dry vermouth*

---

*100 ml/3 1/2 **fl oz**/6 1/2 tbsp single cream*

---

*a few drops of lemon juice*

---

*white pepper*

---

**1** Lightly salt the fish and dust with a little flour.
**2** Fry on both sides in the butter and olive oil.
**3** Blanch the vegetables and mange-tout separately in boiling salted water. Cool with iced water and drain.
**4** Boil the stock and vermouth down to half quantity. Add the cream and cook until the sauce thickens.
**5** Add the vegetables and mange-tout and season with salt, lemon juice and pepper.
**6** Divide the sauce and vegetables between warmed plates and place 1 fish fillet on top of each.

*Photograph (bottom)*

# Gurnard Foil Parcels

Serves 4
Preparation time: 40 mins
1750 kcal/7325 kJ

| |
|---|
| 4 x 300 g/**11 oz** ready-to-cook gurnard |
| salt |
| pepper |
| a few drops of lemon juice |
| 50 g/**2 oz**/¹/₄ cup butter |
| 4 sprigs parsley |
| 4 sprigs rosemary |
| 45 ml/**3 tbsp** white wine |

1  Season the fish with salt and pepper and sprinkle it with lemon juice.
2  Brush melted butter on to 4 sheets of aluminium foil, about 30 x 30 cm (12 x 12 in). Place 1 fish on each sheet and stuff the cavity with some parsley and rosemary. Dot the remaining butter over the outside of the fish.
3  Pour the wine over each fish and close the foil parcel tightly.
4  Bake the fish in a pre-heated oven at 200°C/400°F/gas mark 6 for about 25 minutes.
Variation
Red mullet, gold bream and whiting are also suitable for this recipe.

*Photograph (top)*

---

**Gourmet Tip**
Serve a Saffron Sauce (see page 18) with this dish.

# Tench with Creamy Dill Sauce

Serves 4
Preparation time: 1 hour
1750 kcal/7330 kJ

---

4 x 300 g/**11 oz** tench

salt

1 l/1³/₄ **pts**/4¹/₄ cups fish stock (see page 17)

15 g/¹/₂ **oz**/1 tbsp butter, softened

15 g/¹/₂ **oz**/2 tbsp plain flour

300 ml/¹/₂ **pt**/1¹/₄ cups single cream

2 egg yolks

white pepper

4 sprigs dill, finely chopped

---

1 Gut, clean and dry the fish inside and out. Sprinkle lightly with salt and leave for a few minutes.
2 Bring the fish stock to the boil in a fish steamer, large saucepan or wok fitted with a wire rack. Add the fish.
3 Leave the fish to steam over a low heat for about 20 minutes. Remove carefully and wrap in foil to keep them warm.
4 Take out 500 ml/18 fl oz/2¹/₄ cups stock to make the sauce. Boil it steadily until it has reduced by half and pass it through a sieve.
5 Mix together the butter and flour. Add half the cream to the fish stock, bring to the boil and add the butter and flour paste in pieces, stirring until thickened.

6 Stir the egg yolks into the remaining cream, then stir the mixture into the sauce. Season to taste with salt, pepper and dill.
7 Arrange the tench on warmed plates and coat with some of the sauce. Serve the remaining sauce separately.

*Photograph opposite (top)*

# Trout au Bleu

Serves 4
Preparation time: 30 mins
1550 kcal/6485 kJ

---

4 x 225 g/**8 oz** rainbow trout

30 ml/**2 tbsp** white wine vinegar

salt

75 g/**3 oz**/1¹/₃ cup butter, melted

---

1 If possible, use trout that have just been killed. Clean carefully, ensuring that the skin is intact and still slimy.
2 Pour the vinegar over the fish, ensuring that they have all been well doused.
3 Bring 3 l/5¹/₄ pints of salted water to the boil and gently drop the trout into the pan. Simmer over a gentle heat for about 7 minutes until just done and blue in colour.
4 Remove the fish, dry well on kitchen paper and serve with melted butter.

*Photograph opposite (centre)*

# Plaice with Tomatoes

Serves 4
Preparation time: 40 mins
1700 kcal/7120 kJ

---

8 x 100 g/**4 oz** plaice fillets

salt

a few drops of lemon juice

4 large beef tomatoes

2 cloves garlic

75 ml/**5 tbsp** olive oil

4 shallots, finely chopped

3 sprigs parsley, finely chopped

pepper

---

1 Skin the fillets. Rinse and dry on kitchen paper. Season with salt and lemon juice.
2 Wash the tomatoes, peel, seed and cut into cubes. Peel and crush the garlic.
3 Heat up 60 ml/4 tbsp olive oil and cook 4 fillets at a time on both sides over a medium heat. Remove them from the pan and keep them warm.
4 Fry the shallots in the remaining olive oil until softened, add the tomatoes and garlic and cook for a further 2 minutes. Finally mix in the parsley and season to taste with salt and pepper.
5 Place 2 fillets on each warmed plate and serve with the tomato mixture.
**Variation**
Whiting and gurnard are good for this recipe.

*Photograph opposite (bottom)*

# Herb-Grilled Tuna Steaks

Serves 4
Preparation time: 25 mins
2500 kcal/10460 kJ

| | |
|---|---|
| 100 ml/*3¹/₂ fl oz* olive oil | |
| 5 ml/ *1 tsp* lemon juice | |
| 1 small onion, finely chopped | |
| 1 sprig rosemary, finely chopped | |
| 2 sprigs parsley, finely chopped | |
| 4 bay leaves | |
| pepper | |
| 4 x 225 g/*8 oz* white tuna fish steaks | |
| salt | |

**1** Make a marinade with the oil, lemon juice, onion, chopped herbs, bay leaves and pepper. Leave the tuna steaks to marinate for about 2 hours, turning twice.
**2** Take out the tuna steaks, dab dry and lightly salt. Place on aluminium foil and cook on a low heat under the grill or on the barbecue for about 4 minutes on each side.

*Photograph (top)*

---

**Gourmet Tip**
If the fish is cooked on foil·it will not burn or dry out through contact with the grill pan.

# Eel in Red Wine

Serves 4
Preparation time: 45 mins
2700 kcal/11300 kJ

| |
|---|
| *1 x 1 kg/**2 lb** eel* |
| *salt and white pepper* |
| *a few drops of lemon juice* |
| *450 g/**1 lb** beef tomatoes* |
| *25 g/**1 oz**/2 tbsp butter* |
| *15 g/**¹/₂ oz**/2 tbsp flour* |
| *5 shallots, finely chopped* |
| *100 ml/**3¹/₂ fl oz**/6¹/₂ tbsp red wine (Bordeaux)* |
| *100 ml/**3¹/₂ fl oz**/6¹/₂ tbsp fish stock (see page 17)* |
| *a few sage leaves, cut into strips* |

**1** Buy the eel already skinned from the fishmonger. Cut into pieces about 5 cm/2 in long and clean. Season with salt, pepper and lemon juice.
**2** Skin the beef tomatoes, quarter, seed and cut the flesh into cubes.
**3** Heat up the butter in a saucepan, toss the eel in flour and fry over a low heat, turning frequently.
**4** Add the shallots and tomatoes and cook until softened. Pour in the wine and fish stock, bring to the boil and simmer gently over a low heat for about 20 minutes.
**5** Take out the eel pieces and keep them warm. Add the sage to the sauce, mix in well, and adjust the seasoning. Pour the sauce over the eel.

*Photograph (bottom)*

# Monkfish Rainbow

Serves 4
Preparation time: 50 mins
2680 kcal/11220 kJ

200 g/7 oz red pepper, diced

200 g/7 oz yellow pepper, diced

50 g/2 oz/¼ cup butter

100 ml/3½ fl oz/6½ tbsp fish stock (see page 17)

45 ml/3 tbsp dry vermouth

400 ml/14 fl oz/1¾ cups single cream

salt

a pinch of sugar

white pepper

1 kg/2 lb fresh monkfish

a few drops of lemon juice

flour for dusting

30 ml/2 tbsp olive oil

1 Fry the red and yellow peppers separately in a little butter and pour half the fish stock and vermouth into each pan.
2 Boil to reduce the liquids almost completely, then add equal amounts of cream to each. Cook for a further 5 minutes. Season with salt, sugar and pepper.
3 Mix the peper mixtures separately to a fine purée in an electric blender. Pass through a sieve.
4 Prepare the fish whilst the sauces are cooking.

Remove skin and clean.
5 Cut the fish into 16 medallions, season with salt and lemon juice and lightly dust with flour. Fry in the olive oil and the rest of the butter on both sides over a medium heat for about 2½ minutes.
6 Pour equal amounts of red and yellow pepper sauce on to warmed plates and place the medallions on top.
## Variation
Turbot, brill and halibut are also suitable for this recipe.

# Index of Recipes

Foulsham
Yeovil Road, Slough, Berkshire, SL1 4JH
ISBN 0-572-01663-8
This English language edition copyright
© 1991 W. Foulsham & Co. Ltd.
Originally published by Falken-Verlag,
GmbH, Niedernhausen TS, West
Germany.
Photographs copyright © Falken
Verlag.

All rights reserved.
The Copyright Act (1956) prohibits
(subject to certain very limited
exceptions) the making of copies of any
copyright work or of a substantial part of
such a work, including the making of
copies by photocopying or similar
process. Written permission to make a
copy or copies must therefore normally
be obtained from the publisher in
advance. It is advisable also to consult
the publisher if in any doubt as to the
legality of any copying which is to be
undertaken.

Printed in Portugal.